Meet the Artist™

Paul Cézanne

Melody S. Mis

PowerKiDS
press.
New York

To my fuzzy friends, Cooper, Scooter, and Hans

Published in 2008 by The Rosen Publishing Group, Inc.
29 East 21st Street, New York, NY 10010

First Edition

Editor: Jennifer Way
Book Design: Greg Tucker
Layout Design: Julio Gil
Photo Researcher: Nicole Pristash

Photo Credits: All background images by Shutterstock; cover © Musée d'Orsay, Paris, Lauros/Giraudon/The Bridgeman Art Library; p. 5 © Neue Pinakothek, Munich/The Bridgeman Art Library; p. 6 © Private Collection, Photo © Lefevre Fine Art Ltd., London/The Bridgeman Art Library; p. 9 © Musée Granet, Aix-en-Provence, France, Lauros/Giraudon/The Bridgeman Art Library; p. 11 (top) © Hermitage, St. Petersburg/The Bridgeman Art Library; p. 11 (bottom) © Getty Images; p. 13 © Museu de Arte, Sao Paulo, Giraudon/The Bridgeman Art Library; p. 15 © Kunstmuseum, Basel, Switzerland, Roger-Viollet, Paris/The Bridgeman Art Library; p. 16 © Hermitage, St. Petersburg/The Bridgeman Art Library; pp. 18–19 © Narodni Galerie, Prague, Giraudon/The Bridgeman Art Library; p. 21 © The Barnes Foundation, Merion, Pennsylvania/The Bridgeman Art Library.

Library of Congress Cataloging-in-Publication Data

Mis, Melody S.
  Paul Cézanne / Melody S. Mis. — 1st ed.
    p. cm. — (Meet the artist)
  Includes index.
  ISBN-13: 978-1-4042-3842-8 (library binding)
  ISBN-10: 1-4042-3842-5 (library binding)
  1. Cézanne, Paul, 1839–1906—Juvenile literature. 2. Painters—France—Biography—Juvenile literature. I. Title.
  ND553.C33M57 2008
  759.4–dc22
  [B]
                                                        2007010359

Manufactured in the United States of America

CONTENTS

Meet Cézanne

Paul Cézanne was a French artist. He is famous for his **landscapes** and still-life paintings. Still lifes are paintings of things that do not move, such as apples.

Cézanne is thought of as a postimpressionist artist because he added new ideas to the impressionist **style** of painting. Impressionism is a way of painting that began in the 1860s. The impressionists painted outdoors so they could study the way sunlight changed colors in nature. They were known for using bright colors to paint everyday scenes. This was different from other artists, who often painted historical or biblical scenes.

Cézanne made this self-portrait in the 1870s. A self-portrait is a painting that a person makes of himself or herself. Artists do self-portraits to practice their painting skills or to try out new ways of painting.

5

Provençal Landscape shows the land near Aix, where Cézanne grew up. Cézanne painted many pictures of this part of France during his life.

Young Cézanne

Paul Cézanne was born on January 19, 1839, in a southern French town, called Aix-en-Provence. The land around Aix is filled with mountains and forests. Cézanne loved the Aix countryside and painted many pictures of it during his life.

At age 13, Cézanne went to high school in Aix. There, he met Émile Zola, who would later become a famous writer. The two boys were good friends for most of their lives. When Cézanne was 18 years old, he started taking drawing lessons at an art school in Aix.

Art or Law?

Cézanne's father, Louis-Auguste, was not interested in art. He did not want his son to study art. He wanted Cézanne to be a **lawyer**. In 1859, he sent Cézanne to law school. Cézanne was a good student, but he did not want to be a lawyer. He wanted to be an artist instead.

In 1861, Cézanne quit law school and told his father that he wanted to go to Paris to study art. Louis-Auguste was angry, but in the end he agreed to let Cézanne go. He even gave Cézanne money to live on while he was learning how to paint.

The Dream of the Poet or, The Kiss of the Muse, from 1860, is one of Cézanne's earliest paintings. The Muse, seen on the right, is an imaginary being who gives ideas to artists.

Moving to Paris

In April 1861, Cézanne moved to Paris. His friend Émile Zola was already living there. Cézanne took a test to enter Paris's School of Fine Arts, but he failed it. He then began his art education by painting with other artists at a **studio**. One of the artists at the studio was Camille Pissarro, who painted in the new impressionist style.

Pissarro became an important person in Cézanne's life. He **encouraged** Cézanne to stop painting dark scenes and to start painting colorful scenes from nature using lighter colors.

Top: Girl at the Piano (Overture to Tannhauser), from 1868, is one of the last of Cézanne's early dark paintings.

Right: Cézanne ended his friendship with Zola in the 1880s. He did this because Zola had based a character in one of his books on Cézanne, and Cézanne did not like how that character appeared.

The Impressionists

Cézanne met many impressionist artists through Pissarro. Some of the impressionists thought Cézanne was a strange person because he did not like people to touch him. Others thought he was mean because he often got angry easily.

Cézanne and the impressionists began to send their paintings to the Paris Salon, but they were **rejected**. The salon was the most important art show in Paris. In 1863, Paris held a show for artists whose works had been rejected by the salon. This gave Cézanne and the impressionists a chance to show their paintings to the public.

Portrait of Madame Cézanne in a Red Dress shows Cézanne's longtime girlfriend Marie-Hortense Fiquet. Although she and Cézanne did not marry for many years, she was known as Madame, or Mrs., Cézanne. She is in many of Cézanne's paintings.

Cézanne and Pissarro

In 1870, Cézanne moved to southern France. He returned to Paris a year later and started working on landscapes. Between 1872 and 1874, Cézanne stayed with Pissarro, who had moved to a town outside of Paris.

Pissarro and Cézanne painted outdoors together so they could study nature up close. Cézanne enjoyed painting with Pissarro because Pissarro taught him how to study the way in which sunlight **affected** the colors in nature.

Cézanne showed his paintings at the 1874 and 1877 impressionist **exhibitions** in Paris. Many people laughed at his works because they did not understand them and thought they were terrible.

Cézanne painted *The House of Doctor Gachet at Auvers* in 1873. He painted this house many times and from different sides. Painting the same subject at different times was a way that impressionists studied how light affects how things look. Dr. Gachet was friends with many of the impressionists.

This page: Still Life with Drapery is one of Cézanne's many still lifes. These paintings featured objects from around his house.

Pages 18–19: Jas de Bouffan, from 1887, is one of many views Cézanne painted of his beloved family home in Aix.

Returning to Aix

During the 1880s, Cézanne returned to his hometown of Aix. He liked to paint the country landscapes that he found near his home. His **favorite** scene was a nearby mountain, called Mont Sainte Victoire, which he painted more than 60 times. While he was in Aix, Cézanne began to **create** his own style of painting. He started using larger **sections** of bold colors and different brushstrokes.

In 1886, Cézanne married his longtime girlfriend, Marie-Hortense Fiquet. They had a child, named Paul, who had been born in 1872. Cézanne's father died in 1886. He left the family's house, Jas de Bouffan, to Cézanne.

18

19

A New Style

During the 1890s, Cézanne became interested in showing others how many things in nature had certain **geometric** shapes. For example, to Cézanne, apples looked like balls, and trees were shaped like upside-down ice-cream cones. He began to paint landscapes and objects found in his studio using geometric shapes as guides.

Young artists liked Cézanne's new ideas and often went to Aix to watch him paint. In 1895, the owner of an art store held an exhibition to show Cézanne's geometric works. People were beginning to realize that Cézanne was a great artist.

Cézanne used both geometric shapes and bold colors to paint *The Card Players*, from 1892. You can see that shapes such as circles and rectangles have been shaded, colored, or softened to make the images in this painting.

The Father of Modern Art

During the early 1900s, Cézanne was in bad health, but he worked every day. In October 1906, it started raining while Cézanne was walking to work. He caught a terrible cold and died on October 22.

By the time he died, Cézanne had become a respected artist. He had spent his life trying out new ways to paint everyday scenes and objects. His last works with geometric shapes encouraged other artists to create a new style of painting, which would later be called **modern** art.

GLOSSARY

affected (uh-FEK-ted) Changed.

create (kree-AYT) To produce or to make something.

encouraged (in-KUR-ijd) To have given hope, cheer, or certainty to someone.

exhibitions (ek-suh-BIH-shunz) Shows or displays of objects or pictures that are set out for people to see.

favorite (FAY-vuh-rut) Most liked.

geometric (jee-uh-MEH-trik) Having to do with straight lines, circles, and other shapes.

landscapes (LAND-skayps) Paintings of large sections of land or scenes in nature.

lawyer (LOY-yer) A person who speaks for other people in court.

modern (MO-dern) Using the most up-to-date ideas or ways of doing things. Modern art describes the new ways of making art that were becoming popular in the early twentieth century.

rejected (rih-JEKT-ed) Refused to accept or do something.

sections (SEK-shunz) Parts.

studio (STOO-dee-oh) A room or building where an artist works.

style (STYL) The way in which something is done.

INDEX

WEB SITES

Due to the changing nature of Internet links, PowerKids Press has developed an online list of Web sites related to the subject of this book. This site is updated regularly. Please use this link to access the list: www.powerkidslinks.com/mta/cez/